A Gift for:

_____

Grace and peace be
yours in abundance.
1 Peter 1:2

From:

_____

⧉ ZONDERVAN®

Serenity

Copyright © 2014 by Zondervan

Requests for information should be addressed to:
Zondervan, Grand Rapids, Michigan 49530

ISBN 978-0-310-34242-7

Cover design: Micah Kandros

Interior Photography: © Shutterstock: pages 1–8, 10, 12–13, 15–17, 19–20, 22–24, 26–30, 32–33, 35–37, 39–40, 42–55, 57–60, 62–67, 69–74, 76–77, 79–85, 87–90, 94–101, 103–105, 107, 109–114, 116–118, 121–122, 124, 126–128

Interior Illustrations: Micah Kandros

Interior design: Mallory Perkins

Printed in China

14 15 16 17 18 19 20 /TIMS/ 22 21 20 19 18 17 16 15 14 13 12 11 10 9 8 7 6 5 4 3 2 1

SERENITY

REFLECTIONS AND
SCRIPTURE ON THE
SERENITY PRAYER

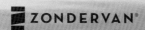

ZONDERVAN®

The Serenity Prayer

God, grant me the serenity
to accept the things I cannot change,
Courage to change the things I can,
and the wisdom to know the difference.
Living one day at a time;
Enjoying one moment at a time;
Accepting hardship as the pathway to peace.
Taking, as he did, this sinful world
as it is, not as I would have it.
Trusting that he will make all things right
if I surrender to his Will;
That I may be reasonably happy in this life,
and supremely happy with him
Forever in the next.
Amen.

—Reinhold Niehbur, 1926

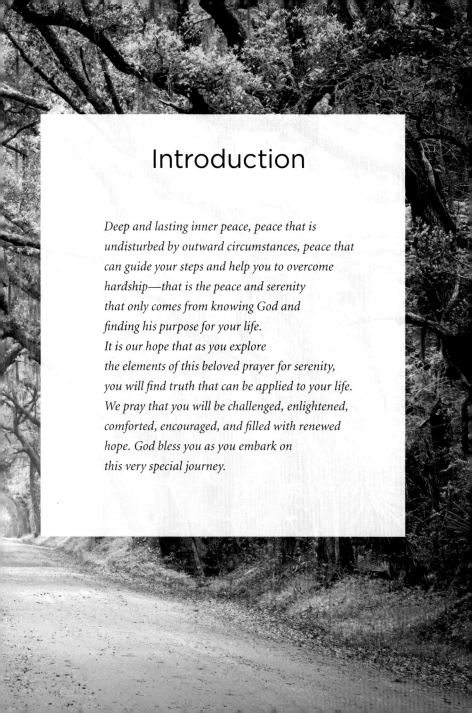

Introduction

*Deep and lasting inner peace, peace that is
undisturbed by outward circumstances, peace that
can guide your steps and help you to overcome
hardship—that is the peace and serenity
that only comes from knowing God and
finding his purpose for your life.
It is our hope that as you explore
the elements of this beloved prayer for serenity,
you will find truth that can be applied to your life.
We pray that you will be challenged, enlightened,
comforted, encouraged, and filled with renewed
hope. God bless you as you embark on
this very special journey.*

God, grant me the serenity
to accept the things I
cannot change . . .

*D*o you long for deep inner peace and serenity? In order to know peace on the outside, you must know it first on the inside. With God's help, you can achieve an internal peace—a spirit that is free from worry and fear—while navigating through an often turbulent and troubled world.

> *Though tempest rage around me*
> *And trouble beset my heart*
> *A peaceful core casts a beam*
> *To pierce the depth of dark.*
> *Transcendent calm that soothes my soul*
> *Comes from divine Abode.*
> *The Lord who is my all in all*
> *Carries my heavy load!*
>
> TARA AFRIAT

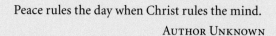

Peace rules the day when Christ rules the mind.

AUTHOR UNKNOWN

The Word of God reveals that true peace comes only from God. It cannot be obtained from any other source. Wealth, human relationships, fame, and fortune cannot produce true and lasting peace—the kind that can see you through tough times.

Christ alone can bring lasting peace—peace with God—peace among men and nations— and peace within our hearts.

BILLY GRAHAM

Who except God can give you peace? Has the world ever been able to satisfy the heart?

GERARD MAJELLA

LORD, You will establish peace for us,
Since You have also performed for us all our works.

ISAIAH 26:12 NASB

God's peace is constant. It isn't subject to the whims of circumstance. It will not rise and fall when trouble comes your way. It will safeguard your heart and give you rest from fear, trouble, and anxiety.

The time of business does not differ from the time of prayer, and in the noise and clutter of my kitchen, while several persons are at the same time calling for different things, I possess God in as great tranquility as if I were upon my knees at the Blessed Sacrament.

BROTHER LAWRENCE

To thee, O God, we turn for peace . . . but grant us too the blessed assurance that nothing shall deprive us of that peace, neither ourselves, nor our foolish earthly desires, nor my wild longings, nor the anxious cravings of my heart.

SØREN AABYE KIERKEGAARD

God's peace is supernatural. It overrides personality and temperament. It is as sure and certain and effective for one person as for another because it comes from the heart of God rather than from the human heart.

> *Drop thy still dews of quietness*
> *Till all our striving cease;*
> *Take from our souls the strain and stress*
> *And let our ordered lives confess*
> *The beauty of thy Peace.*

JOHN GREENLEAF WHITTIER

Where there is peace, God is.

GEORGE HERBERT

God's peace is eternal. It is able to carry you through the entirety of this life and into the next. It won't diminish with time or erode as the years pass. Instead, it will grow even stronger as you give Christ a bigger and bigger place in your life.

> *Like a river glorious*
> *Is God's perfect peace;*
> *Over all victorious*
> *In its bright increase;*
> *Perfect yet it floweth*
> *Fuller every day;*
> *Perfect yet it groweth*
> *Deeper all the way.*
>
> FRANCES RIDLEY HAVERGAL

May the Lord of peace himself give you peace at all times and in every way.

2 Thessalonians 3:16

The first step to receiving God's peace is to make him the center of your life. When you are in charge—you retain the responsibility of finding and maintaining peace for yourself. That burden is a heavy one. If you'll let him, God will carry that burden for you.

For most men the world is centered in self, which is misery: to have one's world centered in God is peace.

Donald Hankey

Nor all my prayers nor sighs nor tears.
Can ease my awful load.
Thy work alone, O Christ
Can ease this weight of sin;
Thy blood alone, O Lamb of God
Can give me peace within.

HORATIUS BONAR

Finding God, you have no need to seek peace, for he himself is your peace.

FRANCES J. ROBERTS

The apostle Paul experienced many trials and tribulations throughout his life. And yet, he describes the peace of God as a peace that transcends all human understanding. He says that you, too, can know that kind of peace, if you are willing to present your requests to God and trust him like Paul did.

Do not be anxious about anything, but in everything, by prayer and petition, with thanksgiving, present your requests to God. And the peace of God, which transcends all understanding, will guard your hearts and minds in Christ Jesus.

PHILIPPIANS 4:6–7

Jesus said, "Peace I leave with you; my peace I give you. I do not give to you as the world gives. Do not let your hearts be troubled and do not be afraid."

JOHN 14:27

No God, no peace. Know God, know peace.

AUTHOR UNKNOWN

Are you searching for peace—the kind of peace that surpasses all understanding? Do you long for serenity strong enough to see you through the darkest nights of your life? Reach out to God. Let him be your strong and constant comfort in the storms that surround you.

> A great windstorm arose, and the waves beat
> into the boat, so that the boat was already being
> swamped. . . . Jesus woke up and rebuked the wind,
> and said to the sea, "Peace! Be still." Then the wind
> ceased, and there was a dead calm.
>
> MARK 4:37, 39 NRSV

> *Even the darkness will not be dark to you;*
> *the night will shine like the day,*
> *for darkness is as light to you.*
>
> PSALM 139:12

If the basis of peace is God, the secret of peace is trust.

J. N. FIGGIS

Many of life's circumstances can be changed when wisdom and determination are applied to them. But there are times when heaven is silent, your resources are depleted, and you are asked to simply "accept" the trial you are facing. At those times, you have an opportunity to realize the depths of God's peace.

"Be still, and know that I am God."

PSALM 46:10

You will keep in perfect peace
him whose mind is steadfast,
because he trusts in you.

ISAIAH 26:3

Acceptance says, *True, this is my situation at the moment. I'll look unblinkingly at the reality of it. But I'll also open my hands to accept willingly whatever a loving Father sends.*

CATHERINE WOOD MARSHALL

When unfortunate circumstances strike your life, you may feel like you're in shock—unable to immediately respond to what is happening. You may feel panic and a sense that your life is out of control.

But your life is never out of control when God is by your side. Reach out for his peace, and it will be waiting.

> The LORD says, "When you pass through the waters,
> I will be with you;
> and when you pass through the rivers,
> they will not sweep over you.
> When you walk through the fire,
> you will not be burned;
> the flames will not set you ablaze."
>
> ISAIAH 43:2

> Even though I walk
> through the valley of the shadow of death,
> I will fear no evil,
> for you are with me.
>
> PSALM 23:4

> "The LORD himself goes before you and will be with you;
> he will never leave you nor forsake you.
> Do not be afraid; do not be discouraged."
>
> DEUTERONOMY 31:8

Anger is also a natural response to troubling circumstances. But left to fester, it will add even more pain to your already struggling heart. Offer your anger to God, and ask him to replace it with his love and grace.

In your anger do not sin;
when you are on your beds,
search your hearts and be silent.

PSALM 4:4

Do not let the sun go down while you are still angry. . . . Get rid of all bitterness, rage and anger.

EPHESIANS 4:26, 31

A fool gives full vent to his anger,
but a wise man keeps himself under control.

PROVERBS 29:11

When tough times come, don't let yourself be overwhelmed by sadness and disappointment. Those emotions are typical, but they will not bring relief to your situation. Surrender your emotions to God, and rejoice as he brings sunlight in the midst of the storm.

I was overcome by trouble and sorrow.
Then I called on the name of the LORD:
"O LORD save me!"
The LORD is gracious and righteous;
our God is full of compassion.
The LORD protects the simplehearted;
when I was in great need, he saved me.

PSALM 116:3–6

Jesus said, "Father, if you are willing, take this cup from me; yet not my will, but yours be done."

LUKE 22:42

The happiest, sweetest, tenderest homes are not those where there has been no sorrow, but those which have been overshadowed with grief, and where Christ's comfort was accepted.

JOHN R. MILLER

Why are you downcast, O my soul? . . .
Put your hope in God,
for I will yet praise him,
my Savior and my God.

PSALM 42:5–6

Accepting the things you cannot change may be one of the most difficult determinations you will ever make. Your first response may be to try to find a way out of your difficulty. But sometimes you will be facing difficulties caused by the choices of others—a child's rebellion, a spouse's betrayal, even the unexpected devastation of an accident or a crime. The only thing you will be able to change is the way you respond.

He does not need to transplant us into a different field, but right where we are, with just the circumstances that surround us, he makes his sun to shine and his dew to fall upon us, and transforms the very things that were before our greatest hindrances into the chiefest and most blessed means of our growth.

HANNAH WHITALL SMITH

Keep your face to the sunshine and you cannot see the shadows.

HELEN KELLER

Whenever you face trials of any kind, consider it
nothing but joy, because you know that the testing
of your faith produces endurance; and let endurance have its full effect, so that you may be mature
and complete, lacking in nothing.

JAMES 1:2–4 NRSV

Many things happen in life that aren't fair—illness, injury, for
example. Accepting those situations means focusing your strength
and energy on releasing yourself to God and letting him see you
through them rather than letting anger, bitterness, sadness, and self-
pity hold you in their grasp.

We know that all things work together for good
to them that love God, to them who are the called
according to his purpose.

ROMANS 8:28 KJV

Be joyful always; pray continually; give thanks in
all circumstances, for this is God's will for you in
Christ Jesus.

1 THESSALONIANS 5:16–18

Jesus wished to avoid the cross and the painful reality of sacrifice for our sins. He asked his Father to let the cup of suffering and
death pass from him. But he could not avoid what was ahead. Later,
as he hung on the cross of Calvary, he said, "Father, into your hands
I commit my spirit" (Luke 23:46).

I can do everything through him who gives me strength.

PHILIPPIANS 4:13

He has not despised or disdained
the suffering of the afflicted one;
he has not hidden his face from him
but has listened to his cry for help.

PSALM 22:24

Jesus, through no fault of his own, suffered the pain and indignity of abuse and death on the cross. When God did not offer a way out, he accepted his destiny without anger or bitterness. He could have marshaled the angels of heaven to rescue him-but he did not!

If you are willing and obedient,
you will eat the best from the land.

ISAIAH 1:19

Which does the Lord prefer: obedience or offerings and sacrifices? It is better to obey him than to sacrifice the best sheep to him.

1 SAMUEL 15:22 GNT

If anyone obeys [the word of Jesus Christ], God's love is truly made complete in him. This is how we know we are in him: Whoever claims to live in him must walk as Jesus did.

1 JOHN 2:5–6

Jesus trusted his Father's wisdom and released himself into his Father's care. In so doing, he turned the tables on the powers and principalities that sought to destroy him. The tomb could not contain him. And the angels of God reported his victory as they stood atop the huge stone that had blocked the entrance to his burial place.

The angel said to the women, "Do not be afraid, for I know that you are looking for Jesus, who was crucified. He is not here; he has risen, just as he said."

MATTHEW 28:5–6

Trust in the LORD with all your heart
and lean not on your own understanding;
in all your ways acknowledge him,
and he will make your paths straight.

PROVERBS 3:5–6

Trust the past to God's mercy, the present to his love, and the future to his providence.

AUGUSTINE OF HIPPO

Jesus accepted what he could not change and was able to reign victorious over his circumstances—the cross. And because he conquered the cross, it is now possible for you to pass through your circumstances with the same sense of peace and shout of victory.

Thanks be to God, who in Christ always leads us in triumphal procession.

2 CORINTHIANS 2:14 NRSV

Everyone born of God overcomes the world. This is the victory that has overcome the world, even our faith.

1 JOHN 5:4

Thanks be to God! He gives us the victory through our Lord Jesus Christ.

1 CORINTHIANS 15:57

If, by the trespass of the one man, death reigned through that one man, how much more will those who receive God's abundant provision of grace and of the gift of righteousness reign in life through the one man, Jesus Christ.

ROMANS 5:17

Of course, there is one more matter to consider. The pain and suffering you are facing may be the direct result of your own poor choices. Even though you may regret those choices, you are unable to change them, and now you are struggling with the consequences. In this too, you must release yourself and your mistakes to God. God's peace and presence will support and comfort you.

> If we claim to be without sin, we deceive ourselves
> and the truth is not in us. If we confess our sins, he
> is faithful and just and will forgive us our sins and
> purify us from all unrighteousness.
>
> 1 JOHN 1:8–9

> The God of all grace, who called you to his eternal
> glory in Christ, after you have suffered a little
> while, will himself restore you and make you
> strong, firm and steadfast.
>
> 1 PETER 5:10

This is what the LORD says:
"If you repent, I will restore you that you may serve me."
                                        JEREMIAH 15:19

A mountain immovable, a swiftly encroaching sea,
Disparate forces of life intent on assailing me.
But, like the oak or ash tossed in egregious storm
Still standing arms up-stretched as if to praise the One
Who controls both gale and sunbeam
And gives strength to continue on.
There is a life deep hid in God
Where all is calm and still,
Where, listening to His holy Word,
One learns to trust, until
All anxious care is put away
And there is peace, profound, always!
Grant us Thy peace, O God!

                                        HENRY W. FROST

God, grant me the courage
to change the things I
can, and the wisdom to
know the difference.

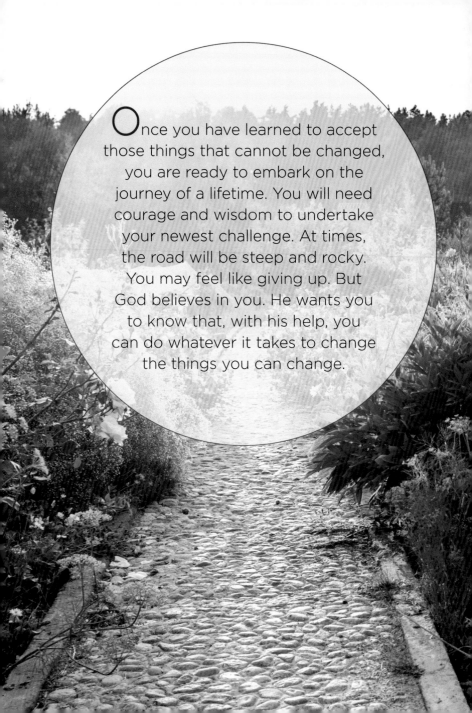

Once you have learned to accept those things that cannot be changed, you are ready to embark on the journey of a lifetime. You will need courage and wisdom to undertake your newest challenge. At times, the road will be steep and rocky. You may feel like giving up. But God believes in you. He wants you to know that, with his help, you can do whatever it takes to change the things you can change.

The Lord said, "Have I not commanded you? Be strong and courageous. Do not be terrified; do not be discouraged, for the Lord your God will be with you wherever you go."

JOSHUA 1:9

"So do not fear, for I am with you;
do not be dismayed, for I am your God.
I will strengthen you and help you;
I will uphold you with my righteous right hand."

ISAIAH 41:10

The changes that need to be made in your life are probably already known to you. You have not been given the power to change others—but you can change yourself. Ask God for the courage to face your own shortcomings. It is his desire to help you change your weakness to strength, your vulnerabilities to victory.

If anyone is in Christ, he is a new creation; the old has gone, the new has come!

2 CORINTHIANS 5:17

Do not conform yourselves to the standards of this world, but let God transform you inwardly by a complete change of your mind.

ROMANS 12:2 GNT

The Lord is my strength and my shield;
my heart trusts in him, and I am helped.

PSALM 28:7

God . . . is not in the business of helping the humanly strong become stronger; rather he takes the weak and makes them strong in himself.

ERWIN W. LUTZER

The apostle Paul struggled with his weaknesses. But at last, he stood settled and secure on this promise from God, his Father: "My grace is sufficient for you, for my power is made perfect in weakness" (2 Corinthians 12:9). God's grace is sufficient for your life too. When you ask God for courage to face your shortcomings, he will be there to give it, without hesitation.

My comfort in my suffering is this:
Your promise preserves my life.

PSALM 119:50

All men who live with any degree of serenity live by some assurance of grace.

REINHOLD NIEBUHR

Grace is the central invitation to life and the final word. It's the beckoning nudge and the overwhelming, undeserved mercy that urges us to change and grow, and then gives us the power to pull it off.

TIM HANSEL

It's likely that you already know the nature of your most grievous shortcoming. It might be something as simple and common as selfishness or as overwhelming as an addiction to alcohol or drugs. In God's eyes, one is no worse than the other. All such attitudes and behaviors cause his beloved children to fall short of the glory of God he intended to be manifested in their lives.

> All sins are attempts to fill voids.
>
> SIMONE WEIL

> Everyone has sinned. No one measures up to God's glory. The free gift of God's grace makes all of us right with him. . . . So he forgives the sins of those who have faith in his blood.
>
> ROMANS 3:23–25 NIrV

> I want you to know that through Jesus the forgiveness of sins is proclaimed to you. Through him everyone who believes is justified.
>
> ACTS 13:38–39

Acknowledging your obvious shortcomings—those things that have caused chaos and confusion in your life—is the first step to peace and healing. Begin with what you know and trust God.

> *He guides the humble in what is right*
> *and teaches them his way.*
>
> PSALM 25:9

I acknowledged my sin to you
and did not cover up my iniquity.
I said, "I will confess
my transgressions to the LORD"—
and you forgave
the guilt of my sin.

PSALM 32:5

[Wisdom's] ways are pleasant ways,
and all her paths are peace.

PROVERBS 3:17

A fault which humbles a man is of more use to him
than a good action which puffs him up.

THOMAS WILSON

When acknowledging your shortcomings, don't give way to guilt or shame. All human beings are imperfect and in need of help and forgiveness. God knows what you are made of, and he has already provided the remedy through the sacrifice of his Son, Jesus Christ. When you stand before him, shortcomings in hand, he will freely forgive.

Have mercy upon me, O God, according to thy loving-
kindness: according unto the multitude of thy tender
mercies blot out my transgressions.
Wash me thoroughly from mine iniquity, and cleanse me
from my sin.

PSALM 51: 1–2 KJV

There is now no condemnation for those who are
in Christ Jesus, because through Christ Jesus the
law of the Spirit of life set me free from the law of
sin and death.

ROMANS 8:1–2

Condemn the fault, and not the actor of it.

WILLIAM SHAKESPEARE

Whatever it is—that shortcoming that has caused you difficulty
and distress—pause right now and ask God to give you the courage to face up to it and destroy its power over you. Name it out loud
and with God's help, bring to your mind specific instances when that
shortcoming has caused pain and suffering for you and others.

Sin shall not be your master, because you are not under law, but under grace.

ROMANS 6:14

Christ's death on the cross included a sacrifice for all our sins, past, present, and future. Every sin that you will ever commit has already been paid for. All of our sins were future when Christ died two thousand years ago. There is no sin that you will ever commit that has not already been included in Christ's death.

ERWIN W. LUTZER

Now picture yourself standing before God's throne—a defendant who has been found guilty and is about to receive the appropriate sentence from the presiding judge. God, the Judge of all the earth, says for you to rise, and as you do so, your lawyer, your advocate, your defender, Jesus Christ, rises with you. Together, you hear the judge's words, "You are free to go," he says. "Your sentence has been paid in full by the one who stands at your side."

> I write this to you so that you will not sin. But if anybody does sin, we have one who speaks to the Father in our defense—Jesus Christ, the Righteous One.
>
> 1 JOHN 2:1

> Is Christ thy advocate to plead thy cause? Art thou his client? Such shall never slide. He never lost his case.
>
> EDWARD TAYLOR

Those words mean that you have been forgiven—completely! The failings of the past have no more power over you. You have courageously changed what could be changed—your own condition. Take some time to bask in the joy of your newfound freedom.

> I will live in perfect freedom,
> because I try to obey your teachings.
>
> PSALM 119:45 GNT

> It is for freedom that Christ has set us free. Stand firm, then, and do not let yourselves be burdened again by a yoke of slavery.
>
> GALATIANS 5:1

> Freedom does not mean I am able to do whatever I want to do. That's the worst kind of bondage. Freedom means I have been set free to become all that God wants me to be, to achieve all that God wants me to achieve, to enjoy all that God wants me to enjoy.
>
> WARREN W. WIERSBE

Once you have courageously handled the obvious sins and shortcomings in your life and submitted them to God, you have reached a milestone. You have taken the first steps toward victory. Will you struggle with those failings in the future? Of course. You struggled to break free, and now you will struggle to stay free. But now you understand the nature of the battle and that Jesus Christ stands with you.

Though we walk in the flesh, we do not war after the flesh: (For the weapons of our warfare are not carnal, but mighty through God to the pulling down of strong holds).

2 CORINTHIANS 10:3–4 KJV

You, dear children, are from God and have overcome them, because the one who is in you is greater than the one who is in the world.

1 JOHN 4:4

The basic test of freedom is perhaps less in what we are free to do than in what we are free not to do.

ERIC HOFFER

Now you are ready to deal with your less obvious failings—the motives that have guided your behaviors, the fears that have kept you feeling hopeless and defeated. Unless these hidden motives are revealed, they will beat against your boat like waves in an angry sea, and your determination to change will be capsized.

> The Lord searches every heart and understands every motive behind the thoughts.
>
> 1 Chronicles 28:9

> The Lord looks out over the whole earth. He gives strength to those who commit their lives completely to him.
>
> 2 Chronicles 16:9 NIrV

> *I will praise the Lord, who counsels me;*
> *even at night my heart instructs me.*
>
> Psalm 16:7

> Some people excuse their faults; others abandon them.
>
> Author Unknown

> You will find it less easy to uproot faults, than to choke them by gaining virtues.
>
> John Ruskin

These motives and fear are often so well-hidden that you may not be able to uncover them without God's help. Spend time in prayer, asking God to expose any way of thinking that needs to be changed. No matter what you are asked to face about yourself, God will be there encouraging you as you take the next step toward changing the things you can change.

> [The LORD] will bring to light what is hidden in darkness and will expose the motives of men's hearts.
>
> 1 CORINTHIANS 4:5

> Jesus said, I have come into the world as a light so that no one who believes in me should stay in darkness."
>
> JOHN 12:46

> Darkness is my point of view, my right to myself; light is God's point of view.
>
> OSWALD CHAMBERS

As each fear, insecurity, and improper motive is revealed, treat it as you have the others. Take responsibility, facing each one with courage and confidence. Then submit each to God, receive his forgiveness and healing. Then rejoice in the wonderful sense of freedom and security that surrounds you.

> Humble yourselves before the Lord, and he will lift you up.
>
> JAMES 4:10

The steadfast love of the LORD never ceases,
his mercies never come to an end;
they are new every morning;
great is your faithfulness.

LAMENTATIONS 3:22–23 NRSV

The voice of sin is loud, but the voice of forgiveness
is louder.

DWIGHT LYMAN MOODY

If God forgives us, we must forgive ourselves.
Otherwise it is almost like setting up ourselves as a
higher tribunal than him.

C. S. LEWIS

God loves you more than you could ever imagine—so much that
he sent his own Son to pay the penalty for your sins and shortcomings. He has ordained a wonderful plan for your life, and he is
filled with joy as he sees you change those things that can be changed
and begin to walk in his purposes for you.

I pray that you, being rooted and established in
love, may have power, together with all the saints,
to grasp how wide and long and high and deep is
the love of Christ.

EPHESIANS 3:17– 18

In [Christ] we have redemption through his blood,
the forgiveness of sins, in accordance with the
riches of God's grace.

EPHESIANS 1:7

"I know the plans I have for you," declares the LORD
"plans to prosper you and not to harm you
plans to give you hope and a future."

JEREMIAH 29:11

You will need God's wisdom in order to walk successfully in your newfound freedoms. The Bible says that God gives that wisdom generously to anyone who asks.

If any of you is lacking in wisdom, ask God, who
gives to all generously and ungrudgingly, and it
will be given you.

JAMES 1:5 NRSV

The way to become wise is to honor the Lord;
he gives sound judgment to all who obey his commands.

PSALM 111:10 GNT

I guide you in the way of wisdom and lead you
along straight paths.

PROVERBS 4:11

Knowledge is horizontal. Wisdom is vertical—it
comes down from above.

BILLY GRAHAM

Resignation is putting God between ourselves and our troubles.

Madame Anne Sophie Soymanov Swetchine

God's wisdom will never lead you down the wrong path. It will keep you from chasing after the expectations of others. It will help you sort through the false hopes and unrealistic solutions in your own mind. Most of all, God's wisdom will keep you on the path to permanent change and eternal victory.

I run in the path of your commands,
for you have set my heart free.

Psalm 119:32

Whether you turn to the right or to the left, your ears will hear a voice behind you, saying, "This is the way; walk in it."

Isaiah 30:21

Men give advice; God gives guidance.

Leonard Ravenhill

Not for one single day
Can I discern my way,
But this I surely know—
Who gives the day,
Will show the way,
So I securely go.

John Oxenham

God has also promised to give you the wisdom to deal with obstacles in your path to permanent change—every stone, every steep and winding incline, every unexpected drop-off, everything along the way is known to him. As you seek his wisdom, he will guide you over, under, around, and through to victory.

> I will lead the blind by ways they have not known,
> along unfamiliar paths I will guide them;
> I will turn the darkness into light before them
> and make the rough places smooth.
>
> ISAIAH 42:16

> [The LORD] leads me beside quiet waters,
> he restores my soul.
> He guides me in paths of righteousness
> for his name's sake.
>
> PSALM 23:2–3

> Be thou a bright flame before me,
> Be thou a guiding star above me,
> Be thou a smooth path below me,
> And be a kindly Shepherd behind me,
> Today, tonight and forever.
>
> ALEXANDER CARMICHAEL

God has given you the victory! He has promised his peace as you tackle the difficult issues of acceptance and change in your life. Look to him for courage as you maintain your victory over the obvious and hidden shortcomings in your life.

Shouts of joy and victory
resound in the tents of the righteous:
"The LORD's right hand has done mighty things!"

PSALM 118:15

The LORD gives strength to his people;
the LORD blesses his people with peace.

PSALM 29:11

The LORD will be your confidence
and will keep your foot from being snared.

PROVERBS 3:26

The triumphant Christian does not fight jar victory; he celebrates a victory already won.

REGINALD WALLIS

God wants us to be victors, not victims; to grow, not grovel; to soar, not sink; to overcome, not to be overwhelmed.

WILLIAM ARTHUR WARD

"As thy day thy strength shall be!"
This should be enough for thee;
He who knows thy frame will spare
Burdens more than thou canst bear.
When thy days are veiled in night,
Christ shall give thee heavenly light;
Seem they wearisome and long,
Yet in him thou shalt be strong.

FRANCES RIDLEY HAVERGAL

Living one day at time; enjoying one moment at a time; accepting hardship as the pathway to peace.

*P*eace, sweet peace! It comes with the assurance of God's love and forgiveness. It comes from knowing that you are in right relationship with him. It comes from living each day in his care.

Since we have been justified through faith, we have peace with God through our Lord Jesus Christ.

ROMANS 5:1

Happy are those whose transgression is forgiven, whose sin is covered.

PSALM 32:1 NRSV

Cast all your anxiety on him because he cares for you.

1 PETER 5:7

At the heart of the cyclone tearing the sky
And flinging the clouds and the towers by
Is a place of central calm;
So here in the roar of mortal things,
I have a place where my spirit sings,
In the hollow of God's palm.

EDWIN MARKHAM

Your determination to accept the things you cannot change and change the things you can will be a daily activity. You may even find that you have to overcome one step at a time. Even when it feels like you are taking one step forward and two steps back, remember that you do not walk alone. God is with you every step of the way.

Do not worry about tomorrow, for tomorrow will worry about itself. Each day has enough trouble of its own.

Matthew 6:34

Our steps are made firm by the Lord,
when he delights in our way;
though we stumble, we shall not fall headlong,
for the Lord holds us by the hand.

Psalm 37:23–24 nrsv

Nothing before, nothing behind;
The steps of faith
Fall on the seeming void, and find
The rock beneath.

John Greenleaf Whittier

Many human achievements are the result of the simple determination to put one foot in front of the other. Mountain climbers take one step, one handhold at a time. They break their rocky opponents into smaller, less-daunting challenges. Small battles win great prizes.

Do you not know that in a race all the runners run, but only one gets the prize? Run in such a way as to get the prize.

1 Corinthians 9:24

I press on toward the goal to win the prize for which
God has called me heavenward in Christ Jesus.

PHILIPPIANS 3:14

The rung of a ladder was never meant to rest upon,
but only to hold a man's foot long enough to enable
him to put the other somewhat higher.

THOMAS HENRY HUXLEY

These remarkable adventurers cannot afford to be distracted
by the elements, the obstacles, or even their own fatigue. They keep
going—one inch, one foot, one victory at a time.

We have fixed our hope on the living God, who is
the Savior of all men, especially of believers.

1 TIMOTHY 4:10 NASB

Let your eyes look directly ahead
And let your gaze be fixed straight in front of you.
Watch the path of your feet
And all your ways will be established.

PROVERBS 4:25–26 NASB

Let us throw off everything that hinders and the sin that so easily entangles, and let us run with perseverance the race marked out for us.

HEBREWS 12:1

When faced with a mountain, I will not quit! I will keep on striving until I climb over, find a pass through, tunnel underneath . . . or simply stay and turn the mountain into a gold mine, with God's help.

ROBERT HAROLD SCHULLER

You will find victory in exactly the same way. Each day you must awaken and recommit yourself to acceptance and action. You cannot afford to be distracted by the opinions of others, your immediate circumstances, or even your own fatigue and discouragement.

> *The fear of others lays a snare,*
> *but one who trusts in the LORD is secure.*
>
> PROVERBS 29:25 NRSV

> *Praise be to the Lord, to God our Savior,*
> *who daily bears our burdens.*
>
> PSALM 68:19

> Jesus said, "If anyone would come after me, he must
> deny himself and take up his cross daily and follow me."
>
> LUKE 9:23

> Living each day as if it were our only day makes for
> a total life lived at full potential.
>
> LLOYD JOHN OGILVIE

> God gives us the ingredients for our daily bread,
> but he expects us to do the baking.
>
> AUTHOR UNKNOWN

Instead, you must keep walking, determinedly, resolutely toward your goal. The wonderful thing is that you have something the average mountain climber does not. At your side and always ready to assist you is God—the one who created you and the very mountain you are trying to climb.

God is our refuge and strength,
an ever-present help in trouble.

PSALM 46:1

I pray that out of his glorious riches he may
strengthen you with power through his Spirit in
your inner being.

EPHESIANS 3:16

The difference between the impossible and the
possible lies in a man's determination.

TOMMY LASORDA

If a blade of grass can grow in a concrete walk and
a jig tree in the side of the mountain cliff, a human
being empowered with an invincible faith can
survive all odds the world can throw against his
tortured soul.

ROBERT HAROLD SCHULLER

As you train your ear to hear his still, small voice above the din of
daily living, you will hear words of encouragement, words of wisdom,
words of love, words that settle you and give you peace. God words!

[Jesus said,] "My sheep listen to my voice; I know
them, and they follow me."

JOHN 10:27

The joy of the LORD is your strength.

NEHEMIAH 8:10

I will listen to what God the LORD will say;
he promises peace to his people, his saints.

PSALM 85:8

Whenever the sounds of the world die out in the
soul, or sink low, then we hear these whisperings
of God. He is always whispering to us, only we do
not always hear because of the noise, hurry, and
distraction which life causes as it rushes on.

FREDERICK WILLIAM FABER

The voice of God is a friendly voice. No one need
fear to listen to it unless he has already made up his
mind to resist it.

A. W. TOZER

As difficult as a mountain climber's challenge might be, despite the cold and the fatigue and the aching muscles, he or she has actually chosen to make the climb. There is an element of enjoyment present in the experience. And you too can find enjoyment in pursuing your challenge.

That everyone may eat and drink, and find satisfaction in all his toil—this is the gift of God .

Ecclesiastes 3:13

You have made known to me the path of life;
you will fill me with joy in your presence,
with eternal pleasures at your right hand.

Psalm 16:11

Things that come to us easily have no significance. Satisfaction comes when we do something difficult; when there is sacrifice involved.

Barry Morris Goldwater

Each day, you will have the pleasure of knowing you made it—you overcame temptation, you refused to give up, you made the changes you could for that day. Already you are a winner! Already you have reason to rejoice!

If Christ is with us, who is against us? You can fight with confidence where you are sure of victory. With Christ and for Christ victory is certain.

St. Bernard of Clairvaux

He conquers who overcomes himself.

LATIN PROVERB

Because [Jesus] himself suffered when he was tempted, he is able to help those who are being tempted.

HEBREWS 2:18

No temptation has seized you except what is common to man. And God is faithful; he will not let you be tempted beyond what you can bear. But when you are tempted, he will also provide a way out so that you can stand up under it.

1 CORINTHIANS 10:13

Was maintaining your victory difficult? Certainly. Was it scary? Of course. Did you execute it perfectly? An unrealistic expectation. The important question is: Did you stay on your feet? And the answer is "Yes." You are a winner because you have survived to climb another day.

I do not ask to walk smooth paths
Nor bear an easy load,
I pray for strength and fortitude
To climb the rock-strewn road.
Give me such courage I can scale
The hardest peaks alone,
And transform every stumbling block
Into a stepping-stone.

GAIL BROOK BURKET

In all these things we are more than conquerors
through him who loved us.

ROMANS 8:37

It is God who arms me with strength
and makes my way perfect.
He makes my feet like the feet of a deer;
he enables me to stand on the heights.

PSALM 18:32–33

You have learned to screen out the human naysayers and the specters from your past. You have learned to depend on God—your traveling companion. You have learned that you have it in you to succeed.

Commit to the LORD whatever you do,
and your plans will succeed.

PROVERBS 16:3

"Forget the former things;
do not dwell on the past.
See, I am doing a new thing . . .
I am making a way in the desert
and streams in the wasteland."

ISAIAH 43:18–19

The past cannot be changed, but our response to it can be.

ERWIN W. LUTZER

No crookedness or deformity in any of your past development, can in the least mar the perfect work that he will accomplish, if you will only put yourselves absolutely into his hands and let him have his own way with you.

HANNAH WHITALL SMITH

The challenge you face each day is a formidable one. It is truly hardship to hold the line and choose to change your life for the better. But it is a hardship that contains great promise of reward.

Do not throw away your confidence; it will be richly rewarded. You need to persevere so that when you have done the will of God, you will receive what he has promised.

HEBREWS 10:35–36

The most rewarding things you do in life are often the ones that look like they cannot be done.

ARNOLD PALMER

After you have suffered for a little while, the God
of all grace, who calls you to share his eternal glory
in union with Christ, will himself perfect you and
give you firmness, strength, and a sure foundation.

1 PETER 5:10 GNT

God's peace is the reward for overcoming the hardship of change.
Once that peace has gripped your heart, the aches and pains of the
day quickly fade away.

Great peace have they who love your law,
and nothing can make them stumble.

PSALM 119:165

The fruit of righteousness will be peace;
the effect of righteousness will be quietness and confidence
forever.
My people will live in peaceful dwelling places,
in secure homes, in undisturbed places of rest.

ISAIAH 32:17–18

Peace does not dwell in outward things, but within
the soul; we may preserve it in the midst of the
bitterest pain if our will remain firm and submis-
sive. Peace in this life springs from acquiescence,
not in an exemption from suffering.

FRANÇOIS DE SALIGNAC DE LA MOTHE FÉNELON

A heart at peace gives life to the body.

PROVERBS 14:30

As you move down the path of change, take time to thank God for helping you stay the course he's called you to. It is because of him that your steps have not slipped from the path to peace.

Since we live by the Spirit, let us keep in step with the Spirit.

GALATIANS 5:25

My steps have held to your paths;
my feet have not slipped.

PSALM 17:5

I will extol you, O LORD, for you have drawn me up
and did not let my foes rejoice over me.

PSALM 30:1 NRSV

Perfection is immutable, but for things imperfect,
to change is the way to perfect them.

OWEN FELTHAM

Today is not yesterday.—We ourselves change.—
How then, can our works and thoughts, if they
are always to be the fittest, continue always the
same.—Change indeed is painful, yet ever needful.

THOMAS CARLYLE

Determine to enjoy every moment of your struggle and your victory over hardship. You've earned it.

> *"I will heal my people and will let them enjoy*
> *abundant peace and security."*
>
> JEREMIAH 33:6

> *Tell the righteous it will be well with them,*
> *for they will enjoy the fruit of their deeds.*
>
> ISAIAH 3:10

> Dear friend, I pray that you may enjoy good health
> and that all may go well with you, even as your soul
> is getting along well.
>
> 3 JOHN v.2

> *The reward of humility and the fear of the LORD*
> *Are riches, honor and life.*
>
> PROVERBS 22:4 NASB

> Whatever can lead an intelligent being to the
> exercise or habit of mental enjoyment, contributes
> more to his happiness than the highest sensual or
> mere bodily pleasures.
>
> THOMAS C. HALIBURTON

Most of all, remember that change is hard work, but the prize for enduring is sweet peace and the knowledge that you have pleased your heavenly Father!

[Jesus said,] "I have told you this so that you will have peace by being united to me. The world will make you suffer. But be brave! I have defeated the world!"

JOHN 16:33 GNT

"My unfailing love for you will not be shaken nor my covenant of peace be removed,"
says the LORD, who has compassion on you.

ISAIAH 54:10

I have fought the good fight, I have finished the race, I have kept the faith. Now there is in store for me the crown of righteousness.

2 TIMOTHY 4:7–8

This is the secret of joy. We shall no longer strive for our own way, but commit ourselves, easily and simply, to God's way, acquiesce in his will, and in so doing find our peace.

EVELYN UNDERHILL

We bless Thee for Thy peace, O God,
Deep as th' unfathomed sea,
Which falls like sunshine on the road
Of those who trust in Thee.
O Father, give our hearts this peace,
Whate'er may outward be,
Till all life's discipline shall cease,
And we go home to Thee.

AUTHOR UNKNOWN

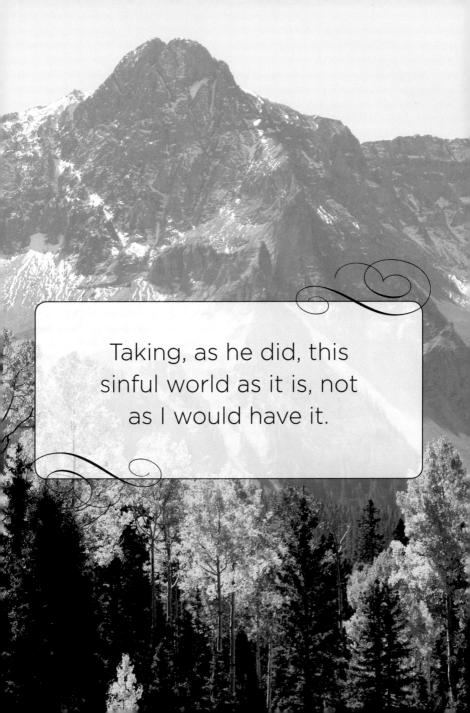

Taking, as he did, this sinful world as it is, not as I would have it.

When you leave this life and gaze into the face of Christ for the first time, you will have reached the end of your journey to perfect peace and serenity. Until then, your struggle, your progress, your victory, your reward will be measured in moments, hours, and days.

> Our struggle is not against flesh and blood, but against the . . . spiritual forces of evil in the heavenly realms.
>
> EPHESIANS 6:12

> If there is no struggle, there is no progress.
>
> FREDERICK AUGUSTUS
> WASHINGTON BAILEY DOUGLASS

> Life is a hard fight, a struggle, a wrestling with the principle of evil, hand to hand, foot to foot. Every inch of the way is disputed. The night is given us to take breath and to pray, to drink deep at the fountain of power. The day, to use the strength that has been given us, to go forth to work with it till the evening.
>
> FLORENCE NIGHTINGALE

Jesus faced the same situation during his time here on earth. He knew the nature of his ultimate mission—the purpose for which he had been sent—but the footsteps he had to take between the cradle and the cross were more difficult to identify and respond to.

Being found in appearance as a man,
[Jesus] humbled himself
and became obedient to death—
even death on a cross!

PHILIPPIANS 2:8

Consider him who endured such opposition from sinful men, so that you will not grow weary and lose heart.

HEBREWS 12:3

Christ suffered for you, leaving you an example, that you should follow in his steps.

1 PETER 2:21

Jesus Christ's outward life was densely immersed in the things of the world, yet he was inwardly disconnected. The one irresistible purpose of his life was to do the will of his Father.

OSWALD CHAMBERS

Jesus stayed on the right path by winning one battle at a time, taking one step at a time, making one good choice at a time. And he did that by staying in constant, vital communication with God, his Father.

> We do not have a high priest who is unable to sympathize with our weaknesses, but we have one who has been tempted in every way, just as we are—yet was without sin.
>
> HEBREWS 4:15

> After he had dismissed [the crowd], he went up on a mountainside by himself to pray. When evening came, he was there alone.
>
> MATTHEW 14:23

> Prayer unites the soul to God.
>
> JULIAN OF NORWICH

> God puts his ear so closely down to your lips that he can hear your faintest whisper. It is not God away off up yonder; it is God away down here, close up.
>
> THOMAS DE WITT TALMAGE

Even Jesus, God's very own Son, understood that the world he was entering was filled with confusion, ambiguities, and contradictions. He realized that from his earthly platform, he could easily become disoriented and stray from the course his Father had set for him.

> *Keep me from going the wrong way,*
> *and in your goodness teach me your law.*
>
> PSALM 119:29 GNT

I do not consider my life of any account as dear
to myself, so that I may finish my course and the
ministry which I received from the Lord Jesus.

ACTS 20:24 NASB

He preserves the way of His godly ones. Then you
will discern righteousness and justice And equity
and every good course.

PROVERBS 2:8–9 NASB

There is a time when we must firmly choose the
course we will follow, or the relentless drift of
events will make the decision.

HERBERT V. PRONCHOW

Aviators have often experienced a similar type of disorientation.
Flying into a cloud bank, navigating a storm, or even in the grip of
darkness, pilots have been known to lose their bearings and unin-
tentionally fly their aircrafts straight into the ground. Experienced
aviators have learned that in such situations, they dare not trust their
senses but depend completely on their instruments.

We live by faith, not by sight.

2 CORINTHIANS 5:7

Every man lives by faith, the nonbeliever as well as
the saint; the one by faith in natural laws and the
other by faith in God.

A. W. TOZER

Some trust in chariots and some in horses,
but we trust in the name of the LORD our God.

PSALM 20:7

Faith does not mean believing without evidence.
It means believing in realities that go beyond
sense and sight.

JOHN BAILLIE

Jesus knew that even though he was God Incarnate, trappings of his humanness—his earthly body and instincts—could not be trusted. They had the potential to lead him straight to disaster. It was imperative that he surrender every thought and conversation and action to his Father who could see clearly from his throne in heaven.

We demolish arguments and every pretension
that sets itself up against the knowledge of God
and we take captive every thought to make it
obedient to Christ.

2 CORINTHIANS 10:5

The mind set on the flesh is death, but the mind set
on the Spirit is life and peace, because the mind set
on the flesh is hostile toward God; for it does not
subject itself to the law of God, for it is not even able
to do so.

ROMANS 8:6–7 NASB

No man is free who is a slave to the flesh.

LUCIUS ANNAEUS SENECA

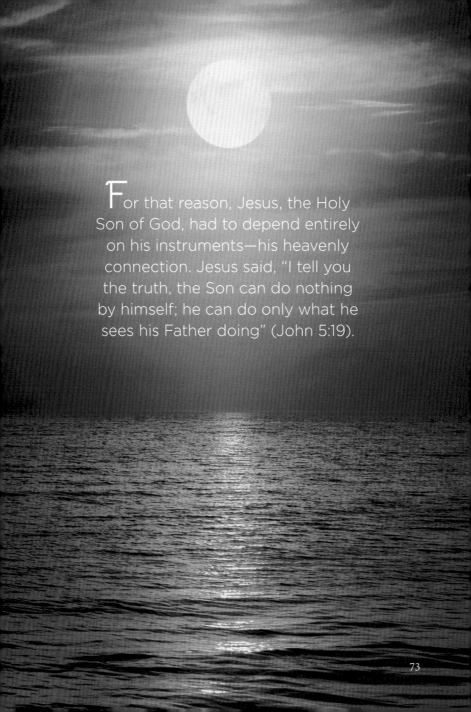

For that reason, Jesus, the Holy Son of God, had to depend entirely on his instruments—his heavenly connection. Jesus said, "I tell you the truth, the Son can do nothing by himself; he can do only what he sees his Father doing" (John 5:19).

My salvation and my honor depend on God;
he is my mighty rock, my refuge.

Psalm 62:7

Trust in the Lord forever,
for the Lord, the Lord, is the Rock eternal.

Isaiah 26:4

Trust in the Lord and do good;
dwell in the land and enjoy safe pasture.

Psalm 37:3

God calls us to live a life we cannot live, so that we
must depend on him for supernatural ability. We
are called to do the impossible, to live beyond our
natural ability.

Erwin W. Lutzer

Jesus accepted the fact that his mission was not to change the world, but to change the hearts of the people within it. In a similar way, God has not chosen to wave his hand and change the world to fit your needs. You will have to walk in the midst of life's storms just as Jesus did. You, too, must accept that you cannot change the world in which you live.

> We, who with unveiled faces all reflect the Lord's glory, are being transformed into his likeness with ever-increasing glory.
>
> 2 CORINTHIANS 3:18

> The expression of Christian character is not good doing, but God-likeness. If the Spirit of God has transformed you within, you will exhibit divine characteristics in your life, not good human characteristics.
>
> OSWALD CHAMBERS

Your success will depend entirely on your ability to understand that your own thoughts and instincts need oversight. They cannot be trusted. Victory in the battle to change what can be changed is achieved only through total dependence upon God—your heavenly connection.

> It is God who works in you to will and to act according to his good purpose.
>
> PHILIPPIANS 2:13

> Let us work as if success depended upon ourselves alone; but with heartfelt conviction that we are doing nothing and God everything.
>
> SAINT IGNATIUS OF LOYOLA

Trust in the Lᴏʀᴅ with all your heart.
Never rely on what you think you know.
Remember the Lᴏʀᴅ in everything you do
and he will show you the right way.
Never let yourself think that you are wiser than you are;
simply obey the Lᴏʀᴅ and refuse to do wrong.

PROVERBS 3:5–7 GNT

Even before Jesus was crucified and resurrected, he told his disciples that he was leaving them with tools—instruments—with which to ensure that their feet would not leave the path to peace. The gifts Jesus left with his followers were both simple and profound. The Bible—the Word of God—would establish a steady foundation, and the Holy Spirit, the third part of the Godhead, would show them how to apply God's Word to their lives.

> [Jesus said,] "It is to your advantage that I go away; for if I do not go away, the Helper will not come to you; but if I go, I will send Him to you."
>
> JOHN 16:7 NASB

> *Your word, O LORD, is eternal;*
> *it stands firm in the heavens.*
>
> PSALM 119:89

> The Spirit of God has the habit of taking the words of Jesus out of their scriptural setting and putting them into the setting of our personal lives.
>
> OSWALD CHAMBERS

Those gifts are available to you today. As you continue to walk day by day and moment by moment . . . choosing to overcome the hardship involved with changing yourself for the better . . . choosing to stay firmly grounded on the path to peace and serenity . . . you must learn to read your instruments.

> The Holy Spirit does not obliterate a man's personality; he lifts it to its highest use.
>
> OSWALD CHAMBERS

The fruit of the Spirit is love, joy, peace, patience,
kindness, goodness, faithfulness, gentleness and
self-control. . . . Those who belong to Christ Jesus
have crucified the sinful nature with its passions
and desires.

GALATIANS 5:22, 24

Cheerfulness keeps up a kind of daylight in the mind
and fills it with a steady and perpetual serenity.

JOSEPH ADDISON

The Bible is much more than a list of religious do's and don'ts. It
is a timeless treasure, penned entirely by men writing under the inspiration of God. It is your guidebook, your manual. It will help you fly
fearlessly even in the darkest storm and the most confusing cloud bank.

All scripture is inspired by God and is useful for
teaching, for reproof, for correction, and for training
in righteousness, so that everyone who belongs to God
may be proficient, equipped for every good work.

2 TIMOTHY 3 :16–17 NRSV

"I do not set aside the grace of God, for if righteousness could be gained through the law, Christ
died for nothing!"

GALATIANS 2:21

For grace is given not because we have done good
works, but in order that we may be able to do them.

SAINT AUGUSTINE OF HIPPO

Open the pages of the Bible at least once every day. Even if you read no more than a few verses or one chapter, your heart will begin to respond. Soon you will find yourself strengthened, fortified, enlivened, established by the Bible's innate wisdom and counsel.

> The word of God is living and active. Sharper
> than any double-edged sword, it penetrates even
> to dividing soul and spirit, joints and marrow; it
> judges the thoughts and attitudes of the heart.
>
> HEBREWS 4:12

> Other books were given for our information, the
> Bible was given for our transformation.
>
> AUTHOR UNKNOWN

*The ordinances of the L*ORD *are sure*
and altogether righteous.
They are more precious than gold,
than much pure gold;
they are sweeter than honey,
than honey from the comb.

PSALM 19:9–10

You will learn to hear the Holy Spirit by quieting your own thoughts and waiting expectantly for his voice within you. Jesus often had to slip away from the crowds, in order to hear his Father's voice. You will probably have to do the same. At least once each day, close your eyes, turn from your own thoughts, and wait on God for guidance and spiritual direction.

They that wait upon the LORD shall renew their strength; they shall mount up with wings as eagles; they shall run, and not be weary; and they shall walk, and not faint.

ISAIAH 40:31 KJV

Wait on the Lord in prayer as you sit on the freeway, sharing with him the anxiety of so many jobs to be done in such a short time. Watch your frustrations melt into praise as you sing hymns and choruses for his ears alone.

JONI EARECKSON TADA

Just as experienced aviators learn to set their senses aside and depend on their instruments, you will need to learn to set aside your earthbound opinions and strategies and wait to receive God's wisdom for each and every situation.

> Everyone who lives on milk, being still an infant, is unskilled in the word of righteousness. But solid food is for the mature, for those whose faculties have been trained by practice to distinguish good from evil.
>
> HEBREWS 5:13–14 NRSV

> *"My thoughts are not your thoughts,*
> *neither are your ways my ways,"*
> *declares the LORD.*
> *"As the heavens are higher than the earth*
> *so are my ways higher than your ways,*
> *and my thoughts than your thoughts."*
>
> ISAIAH 55:8–9

> Faith is not anti-intellectual. It is an act of man that reaches beyond the limits of our five senses.
>
> BILLY GRAHAM

Jesus dealt with the world as it was—sinful and dark. He was victorious because he accepted his circumstances and chose to change what he could change—the hearts of men and women. You may not be able to change the world you live in or the circumstances of your life. But you can change your destiny by placing yourself, your thoughts, your opinions, your actions in God's hands.

Holy brothers, who share in the heavenly calling, fix your thoughts on Jesus, the apostle and high priest whom we confess.

HEBREWS 3:1

"*Submit to God and be at peace with him;*
in this way prosperity will come to you."

JOB 22:21

His love, his judgments are all man's home. To think his thoughts, to choose his will, to love his loves, to judge his judgments, and thus to know that he is in us, is to be at home.

GEORGE MACDONALD

Out of the light that dazzles me,
Bright as the sun from pole to pole,
I thank the God I know to be
For Christ the conqueror of my soul.
Since His the sway of circumstance,
I would not wince nor cry aloud.
Under that rule which men call chance
My head with joy is humbly bowed.
I have no fear, though straight the gate,
He cleared from punishment the scroll.
Christ is the Master of my fate,
Christ is the Captain of my soul.

DOROTHEA DAY

Trusting that God will make all things right if I surrender to his Will.

*G*od's Will—it's a phrase you've probably heard a lot in your life. Just about everything that can't be quickly reasoned out in human terms ends up being relegated to that category. But what does it really mean to be surrendered to God's Will?

> Do not conform any longer to the pattern of this world, but be transformed by the renewing of your mind. Then you will be able to test and approve what God's will is—his good, pleasing and perfect will.
>
> ROMANS 12:2

> Not as I will, but as thou wilt. To be able to say these words and truly mean them is the highest point we can ever hope to attain. Then, indeed, we have broken out of time's hard shell to breathe, not its stale air, but the fresh, exhilarating atmosphere of eternity.
>
> MALCOLM MUGGERIDGE

God's Will is quite simply his plan and purpose—for the world in general and for you specifically. That purpose is the very reason for which you were created.

> *Many are the plans in a man's heart,*
> *but it is the LORD's purpose that prevails.*
>
> PROVERBS 19:21

We are God's workmanship, created in Christ Jesus
to do good works, which God prepared in advance
for us to do.

EPHESIANS 2:10

The plans of the LORD stand firm forever,
the purposes of his heart through all generations.

PSALM 33:11

God would not have created us without a specific
plan in mind.

ERWIN W. LUTZER

God's heavenly plan doesn't always make earthly sense.

CHARLES R. SWINDOLL

Surrendering to God's Will means that you are choosing to walk in harmony with the purposes for which you were created. By what other means could you hope to achieve your highest potential, feel the warmth of personal fulfillment, live life to the fullest?

> [Jesus said,] "I have come that they may have life, and have it to the full."
>
> JOHN 10:10

> The world and its desires pass away, but the man who does the will of God lives forever.
>
> 1 JOHN 2:17

> *O Will, that willest good alone,*
> *Lead thou the way, thou guidest best;*
> *A silent child, I follow on,*
> *And trusting lean upon thy breast.*
> *And if in gloom I see thee not,*
> *I lean upon thy love unknown;*
> *In me thy blessed will is wrought,*
> *If I will nothing of my own.*
>
> GERHARD TERSTEEGEN

You are much more than a cosmic accident or a random inspiration. Is that what you thought? You are a special and unique creation, fashioned by God himself in his own image. In other words, you are one of almighty God's very best ideas!

You created my inmost being; you
knit me together in my mother's womb.
I praise you because I am fearfully and wonderfully made;
your works are wonderful, I know that full well.

PSALM 139:13–14

God created man in his own image,
in the image of God he created him;
male and female he created them.

GENESIS 1:27

Your hands made me and formed me;
give me understanding to learn your commands.

PSALM 119:73

Numberless are the world's wonders, but none
more wonderful than man.

SOPHOCLES

When you were being framed in the mind of God, he was planning for more than the circumstances of your birth. He didn't just make you then toss you out into the world to find your own way. His creative process included a plan and a purpose for your life—his Will for you.

God has never been known to disappoint the man
who is sincerely wanting to cooperate with his own
purposes.

J. B. PHILLIPS

My frame was not hidden from you
when I was made in the secret place.
When I was woven together in the depths of the earth,
your eyes saw my unformed body.
All the days ordained for me
were written in your book
before one of them came to be.

PSALM 139:15–16

From one man he made every nation of men, that
they should inhabit the whole earth; and he deter-
mined the times set for them and the exact places
where they should live.

ACTS 17:26

Only one uncertainty existed in God's plan—and it was of his
own making. God wanted you to choose him just as he had already
chosen you. He could have demanded your love and devotion, but he
did not. He endowed you with your own will—the power to accept
or reject what he had planned.

This day I call heaven and earth as witnesses
against you that I have set before you life and
death. . . . Now choose life, so that you and your
children may live and that you may love the LORD
your God, listen to his voice, and hold fast to him.
For the LORD is your life.

DEUTERONOMY 30:19–20

Faith means being grasped by a power that is greater than we are, a power that shakes us and turns us, and transforms and heals us. Surrender to this power is faith.

Paul Johannes Oskar Tillich

Throughout your life, God, your Creator, has watched over you and waited patiently for the day when you would turn to him and choose to surrender yourself to his wonderful plan for you.

> *From heaven the Lord looks down and*
> *sees all mankind;*
> *from his dwelling place he watches*
> *all who live on earth—*
> *he who forms the hearts of all,*
> *who considers everything they do.*

Psalm 33:13–15

> *I have sought your face with all my heart;*
> *be gracious to me according to your promise.*
> *I have considered my ways*
> *and have turned my steps to your statutes.*

Psalm 119:58–59

Behind the dim unknown standeth God within the shadow, keeping watch above his own.

James Russell Lowell

Regardless of what choices you have made in the past, God is able to plant your feet firmly on that path to peace and serenity. He is able to make all things—the things you cannot change and the things you can—work together for your good. And your good is all he has ever wanted—it is his perfect Will.

> When I said, "My foot is slipping,"
> your love, O LORD, supported me.
>
> PSALM 94:18

> Direct my footsteps according to your word;
> let no sin rule over me.
>
> PSALM 119:133

> My help comes from the LORD,
> the Maker of heaven and earth.
> He will not let your foot slip—
> he who watches over you will not slumber.
>
> PSALM 121:2–3

> If God maintains sun and planets in bright and
> ordered beauty, he can keep us.
>
> F. B. MEYER

As you surrender yourself to God's Will, you should understand that God's purpose for you will likely be revealed over the course of a lifetime. You may be thinking that it would be much easier if God would just lay the details out before you. But he does not.

*The path of the righteous is like the first gleam of dawn,
shining ever brighter till the full light of day.*

PROVERBS 4:18

*Your word is a lamp to my feet
and a light for my path.*

PSALM 119:105

*Show me your ways, O LORD,
teach me your paths;
guide me in your truth and teach me,
for you are God my Savior.*

PSALM 25:4–5

A glimpse of the next three feet of road is more
important and useful than a view of the horizon.

C. S. LEWIS

God's determination to reveal his Will one step at a time is well
conceived. It affords opportunities for you to get to know him, learn
to trust him, and begin to love him—of your own free will.

*[Jesus said,] "I am the good shepherd;
I know my sheep and my sheep know me."*

JOHN 10:14

[Jesus prayed,] "This is eternal life: that they may
know you the only true God, and Jesus Christ,
whom you have sent."

JOHN 17:3

[Jesus said,] "I will ask the Father, and he will give you another Counselor to be with you forever—the Spirit of truth. The world cannot accept him, because it neither sees him nor knows him. But you know him, for he lives with you and will be in you."

JOHN 14:16–17

Even Jesus walked out God's Will for his life one step at a time. He trusted God to keep him on track and light the path before him. And God was faithful!

> Let the morning bring me word of your unfailing love,
> for I have put my trust in you.
> Show me the way I should go,
> for to you I lift up my soul. . . .
> Teach me to do your will,
> for you are my God;
> may your good Spirit
> lead me on level ground.
>
> PSALM 143:8, 10

> The LORD is your keeper;
> The LORD is your shade on your right hand.
> The sun will not smite you by day,
> Nor the moon by night.
> The LORD will protect you from all evil;
> He will keep your soul.
> The LORD will guard your going out and your coming in
> From this time forth and forever.
>
> PSALM 121:5–8 NASB

The path that Jesus walked took him to the Cross, through the Cross, and beyond it. As each step was revealed, Jesus submitted his own will to God's—even when it meant great hardship.

> *The Sovereign LORD has opened my ears,*
> *and I have not been rebellious;*
> *I have not drawn back.*
> *I offered my back to those who beat me,*
> *my cheeks to those who pulled out my beard;*
> *I did not hide my face*
> *from mocking and spitting.*
> *Because the Sovereign LORD helps me,*
> *I will not be disgraced.*
> *Therefore have I set my face like flint,*
> *and I know I will not be put to shame.*

ISAIAH 50:5–7

Independence is not strength but unrealized weakness and is the very essence of sin. There was no independence in our Lord, the great characteristic of his life was submission to his Father.

OSWALD CHAMBERS

The Bible says that in the Garden of Gethsemane, Jesus was in such agony that he sweat drops of blood. He asked his Father if there might be another way to accomplish the mission for which he had been sent.

> [Jesus said,] "Now my heart is troubled, and what shall I say? 'Father, save me from this hour'? No, it was for this very reason I came to this hour. Father, glorify your name!" Then a voice came from heaven, "I have glorified it, and will glorify it again."
>
> JOHN 12:27–28

[Jesus] fell with his face to the ground and prayed, "My Father, if it is possible, may this cup be taken from me. Yet not as I will, but as you will."

MATTHEW 26:39

Jesus Christ's outward life was densely immersed in the things of the world, yet he was inwardly disconnected. The one irresistible purpose of his life was to do the will of his Father.

OSWALD CHAMBERS

God did not spare him the hardship, but urged Jesus on for your sake. Jesus' destiny was to suffer for your sins and those of all mankind. The humanness in Jesus struggled in the Garden to avoid the suffering of the cross, but he trusted his heavenly Father and pushed forward to accomplish his mission.

Let us fix our eyes on Jesus, the author and perfecter of our faith, who for the joy set before him endured the cross scorning its shame, and sat down at the right hand of the throne of God.

HEBREWS 12:2

I do not think that prayer is ever evasion, that prayer saves us from having to face things that we do not want to face and that are going to hurt if we face them. Jesus in Gethsemane discovered that there was no evasion of the cross.

WILLIAM BARCLAY

In the midst of his suffering, Jesus committed his spirit to God and surrendered fully to God's Will. His obedience won him victory even over death. On Resurrection Sunday, hardship gave way to peace and serenity for the Son of God.

> Jesus called out with a loud voice, "Father, into your hands I commit my spirit." When he had said this, he breathed his last.
>
> LUKE 23:46

> "Death has been swallowed up in victory."
> "Where, O death, is your victory?
> Where, O death, is your sting?" . . .
> But thanks be to God! He gives us the victory through our Lord Jesus Christ.
>
> 1 CORINTHIANS 15:54–55, 57

> The same power that brought Christ back from the dead is operative within those who are Christ's. The Resurrection is an ongoing thing.
>
> LEON MORRIS

Jesus rose from the grave and took his place at the right hand of his heavenly Father. He had trusted, endured, overcome. And as he surrendered to God's Will, his faithful Father had made things right for him—just as he had promised.

> [Jesus said,] "In this world you will have trouble. But take heart! I have overcome the world."
>
> JOHN 16:33

This power working in us is the same as the mighty strength which he used when he raised Christ from the dead and seated him at his right side in the heavenly world.

EPHESIANS 1:19–20 GNT

The Son is the radiance of God's glory and the exact representation of his being, sustaining all things by his powerful word. After he had provided purification for sins he sat down at the right hand of the Majesty in heaven.

HEBREWS 1:3

God wants to make things right for you too. But first you may be asked to endure the hardship of change in your life. No matter what you are facing, move forward with confidence. God is with you. He has promised never to leave you. Commit yourself to him and walk on to victory.

Endure hardship with us like a good soldier of Christ Jesus. No one serving as a soldier gets involved in civilian affairs—he wants to please his commanding officer.

2 TIMOTHY 2:3–4

The LORD loves the just
and will not forsake his faithful ones.
They will be protected forever.

PSALM 37:28

God has said, "Never will I leave you;
never will I forsake you."
So we with confidence,
"The Lord is my helper; I will not be afraid.
What can man do to me?"

HEBREWS 13:5–6

Thy way, not mine, O Lord,
However dark it be!
Lead me by thine own hand,
Choose out the path for me.
Not mine, not mine the choice,
In things great or small;
Be thou my guide, my strength,
My wisdom and my all!

HORATIUS BONAR

That I may be reasonably happy in this life, and supremely happy with him forever in the next. Amen.

*D*oes true happiness really exist in this life? The Bible says that Moses found it by turning his back on the riches of Egypt and becoming the fierce leader of the Israelite nation.

> By faith Moses, when he had grown up, refused
> to be known as the son of Pharaoh's daughter. He
> chose to be mistreated along with the people of
> God rather than to enjoy the pleasures of sin for
> a short time. He regarded disgrace for the sake
> of Christ as of greater value than the treasures of
> Egypt, because he was looking ahead to his reward.
>
> HEBREWS 11:24–26

> *You have to be willing to change and obey me.*
> *If you are, you will eat the best food that grows on the land.*
>
> ISAIAH 1:19 NIrV

The apostle Paul found contentment within the confines of a prison cell as he penned the letters that would one day make up a good portion of the New Testament.

> I, Paul, am writing this greeting with my own
> hand. Remember that I am being held by chains.
>
> COLOSSIANS 4:18 NIrV

> About midnight Paul and Silas were praying. They
> were also singing hymns to God. The other prisoners
> were listening to them.
>
> ACTS 16:25 NIrV

I have learned to be content whatever the circumstances. I know what it is to be in need, and I know what it is to have plenty. I have learned the secret of being content in any and every situation, whether well fed or hungry, whether living in plenty or in want. I can do everything through him who gives me strength.

PHILIPPIANS 4:11–13

Mother Teresa, a great woman of God, found happiness in the touch of a dying beggar on the streets of Calcutta, India.

> *"Happy are those who are merciful to others;*
> *God will be merciful to them!*
> *Happy are the pure in heart;*
> *they will see God!*
> *Happy are those who work for peace;*
> *God will call them his children!"*

MATTHEW 5:7–9 GNT

We all long for heaven where God is, but we have it in our power to be in heaven with him right now—to be happy with him at this very moment. But being happy with him now means:

> loving as he loves,
> helping as he helps,
> giving as he gives,
> serving as he serves,
> rescuing as he rescues,
> being with him for all the twenty-four hours.

MOTHER TERESA OF CALCUTTA

All of these people believed that happiness and fulfillment could be found by pursuing God's Will—his specific purpose and plan for them. They turned over the moments, the hours, the days of their lives to pursuing the plan for which they had been created.

> God leads us step by step, from event to event.
> Only afterwards, as we look back over the way
> we have come and reconsider certain important
> moments in our lives in the light of all that has
> followed them, . . . or when we survey the whole
> progress of our lives, do we experience the feeling
> of having been led without knowing it, the feeling
> that God has mysteriously guided us.
>
> PAUL TOURNIER

Commit your way to the LORD;
trust in him, and he will act.

PSALM 37:5 NRSV

Commit to the LORD whatever you do,
and your plans will succeed.

PROVERBS 16:3

Moses, Paul, and Mother Teresa experienced hardship, but it did not stop them. They embraced it and trusted God to make things right for them.

Those who suffer according to God's will should commit themselves to their faithful Creator and continue to do good.

1 PETER 4:19

We are hard pressed on every side, but not crushed; perplexed, but not in despair; persecuted, but not abandoned; struck down, but not destroyed.

2 Corinthians 4:8–9

Christ made no promise that those who followed him in his plan of re-establishing life on its proper basic principles would enjoy a special immunity from pain and sorrow—nor did he himself experience such immunity. He did, however, promise enough joy and courage, enough love and confidence in God to enable those who went his way to do far more than survive.

J. B. Phillips

Many have found that true happiness comes from doing those things for which they were created, living in harmony with God's Will for their lives.

*If you spend yourselves in behalf of the hungry
and satisfy the needs of the oppressed,
then your light will rise in the darkness,
and your night will become like the noonday.
The LORD will guide you always;
he will satisfy your needs in a sun-scorched land and will
strengthen your frame.
You will be like a well-watered garden,
like a spring whose waters never fail.*

ISAIAH 58:10–11

If you have received the Spirit and are obeying him,
you find he brings your spirit into complete harmony with God, and the sound of your goings and
the sound of God's goings are one and the same.

OSWALD CHAMBERS

Your happiness will also be found in following God's plan for
your life. You will experience the deep inner happiness of knowing
that your feet are firmly planted on the path to peace and serenity
and the satisfaction of knowing that you are fulfilling your destiny.

"Call to me, and I will answer you; I will tell you
wonderful and marvelous things that you know
nothing about."

JEREMIAH 33:3 GNT

"I know the plans I have for you," announces the Lord. "I want you to enjoy success. I do not plan to harm you. I will give you hope for the years to come."

JEREMIAH 29:11 NIrV

Until we have learned to be satisfied with fellowship with God, until he is our rock and our fortress, we will be restless with our place in the world.

ERWIN W. LUTZER

The Bible says that God has prepared a place for those who surrender their wills to his. In the Bible, Jesus told his disciples all about it.

[Jesus said,] "Do not let your hearts be troubled. Trust in God; trust also in me. In my Father's house are many rooms; if it were not so, I would have told you. I am going there to prepare a place for you. And if I go and prepare a place for you, I will come back and take you to be with me that you also may be where I am. You know the way to the place where I am going."

JOHN 14:1–4

Now we know that if the earthly tent we live in is destroyed, we have a building from God, an eternal house in heaven, not built by human hands.

2 CORINTHIANS 5:1

Jesus also told his disciples that they would continue there for eternity. Death and tears and hardship and suffering would be banished from that place. Life and peace and truth and love would reign in his kingdom without end.

> *"The Lamb at the center of the throne will be their shepherd;*
> *he will lead them to springs of living water.*
> *And God will wipe away every tear from their eyes."*
>
> REVELATION 7:17

[John] heard a loud voice from the throne saying, "Now the dwelling of God is with men, and he will live with them. They will be his people, and God himself will be with them and be their God. He will wipe every tear from their eyes. There will be no more death or mourning or crying or pain, for the old order of things has passed away."

REVELATION 21:3–4

Imagine! After living your life in communion with your Creator and accomplishing the purpose for which you were created, you will find that your happiness has just begun. Complete and full, it will continue for eternity in his presence.

> Jesus said, "Behold, I am coming soon! My reward is with me, and I will give to everyone according to what he has done."
>
> REVELATION 22:12

> I have fought the good fight, I have finished the race, I have kept the faith. Now there is in store for me the crown of righteousness, which the Lord, the righteous Judge will award to me on that day—and not only to me, but also to all who have longed for his appearing.
>
> 2 TIMOTHY 4:7–8

> *There is a land of pure delight,*
> *Where saints immortal reign;*
> *Infinite day excludes the night.*
> *And pleasures banish pain.*
>
> ISAAC WATTS

> *Come, Lord, when grace has made me meet*
> *Thy blessed face to see;*
> *For if thy work on earth be sweet*
> *What will thy glory be!*
> *My knowledge of that life is small*
> *The eye of faith is dim;*
> *But 'tis enough that Christ knows all*
> *And I shall be with him.*
>
> RICHARD BAXTER

Questions for Reflection

*W*ill you allow your loving Creator to help you accept the things you cannot change?

Whatever is true, whatever is noble, whatever is right, whatever is pure, whatever is lovely, whatever is admirable—if anything is excellent or praise-worthy—think about such things. Whatever you have learned or received or heard from me, or seen in me—put it into practice. And the God of peace will be with you.

Philippians 4:8–9

For after all, the best thing one can do when it's raining is to let it rain.

Henry Wadsworth Longfellow

I know what it is to be in need and what it is to have more than enough. I have learned this secret, so that anywhere, at any time, I am content, whether I am full or hungry, whether I have too much or too little. I have the strength to face all conditions by the power that Christ gives me.

PHILIPPIANS 4:12–13 GNT

Will you allow God to help you change the things you can?

It is God who is at work in you, both to will and to work for His good pleasure.

PHILIPPIANS 2:13 NASB

Let us draw near with confidence to the throne of grace, so that we may receive mercy and find grace to help in time of need.

HEBREWS 4:16 NASB

I lift up my eyes to the hills—
where does my help come from?
My help comes from the LORD,
the Maker of heaven and earth.

PSALM 121:1–2

Restore to me the joy of your salvation
and grant me a willing spirit, to sustain me.

PSALM 51:12

"Watch and pray so that you will not fall into temptation. The spirit is willing, but the body is weak."

MATTHEW 26:41

Will you trust God's wisdom to help you discern what can be changed in your life and what cannot?

If any of you lacks wisdom, he should ask God,
who gives generously to all without finding fault,
and it will be given to him.

JAMES 1:5

*Those who know your name will trust in you,
for you, LORD, have never forsaken those who seek you.*

PSALM 9:10

*I trust in your unfailing love;
my heart rejoices in your salvation.
I will sing to the LORD,
for he has been good to me.*

PSALM 13:5–6

*To you, O LORD, I lift up my soul;
in you I trust, O my God.
Do not let me be put to shame.*

PSALM 25:1–2

Wisdom is seeing life from God's perspective.

BILL GOTHARD

Will you allow God to help you live one day at a time, enjoying one moment at a time as you walk through the hardship that change requires?

> [Jesus said,] "Do not worry about tomorrow; it will have enough worries of its own. There is no need to add to the troubles each day brings."
>
> MATTHEW 6:34 GNT

> *I am the LORD, your God,*
> *who takes hold of your right hand*
> *and says to you, Do not fear;*
> *I will help you.*
>
> ISAIAH 41:13

[The Lord says,] *"Fear not, for I have redeemed you;*
I have summoned you by name; you are mine.
When you pass through the waters,
I will be with you;
and when you pass through the rivers,
they will not sweep over you.
When you walk through the fire,
you will not be burned;
the flames will not set you ablaze."

ISAIAH 43:1–2

Will you agree to look realistically at the world and realize that you cannot change it, but you can overcome it by letting God change your heart?

Search me, O God, and know my heart;
test me and know my anxious thoughts.
See if there is any offensive way in me,
and lead me in the way everlasting.

PSALM 139:23–24

Who can discern his errors?
Forgive my hidden faults.
Keep your servant also from willful sins;
may they not rule over me.
Then will I be blameless,
innocent of great transgression.
May the words of my mouth and the meditation of my heart
be pleasing in your sight,
O Lord, my Rock and my Redeemer.

PSALM 19:12–14

Test me, O LORD, and try me,
examine my heart and my mind;
for your love is ever before me,
and I walk continually in your truth.

PSALM 26:2–3

Will you choose God as he has chosen you? Will you surrender your will to the one who is able to keep your feet on the pathway to peace?

Jesus said, "You did not choose me, but I chose you and appointed you to go and bear fruit—fruit that will last."

JOHN 15:16

I will praise the LORD, who counsels me;
even at night my heart instructs me.
I have set the LORD always before me.
Because he is at my right hand,
I will not be shaken.

PSALM 16:7–8

You, LORD, give perfect peace
to those who keep their purpose firm
and put their trust in you.

ISAIAH 26:3 GNT

We have all had human fathers who disciplined us and we respected them for it. How much more should we submit to the Father of our spirits and live!

HEBREWS 12:9

Will you commit your life to finding happiness through accomplishing God's plan and purpose for your life?

> Lord, you establish peace for us;
> all that we have accomplished you have done for us.
> O Lord, our God, other lords besides you have ruled over
> us,
> but your name alone do we honor.
>
> Isaiah 26:12–13

> Happy is everyone who fears the Lord,
> who walks in his ways.
> You shall eat the fruit of the labor of your hands;
> you shall be happy, and it shall go well with you.
>
> Psalm 128:1–2 nrsv

> Happy are those who make
> the Lord their trust,
> who do not turn to the proud,
> to those who go astray after false gods.
>
> Psalm 40:4 nrsv

> Happy are those whom you choose and bring near
> to live in your courts.
> We shall be satisfied with the goodness of your house,
> your holy temple.
>
> Psalm 65:4 nrsv

Will you set your thoughts on the promise of eternal happiness—
dwelling in the presence of God forever?

> *You prepare a banquet for me,*
> *where all my enemies can see me;*
> *you welcome me as an honored guest*
> *and fill my cup to the brim.*
> *I know that your goodness and love will be with me all*
> *my life;*
> *and your house will be my home as long as I live.*
>
> PSALM 23:5–6 GNT

> *One thing I ask of the LORD,*
> *this is what I seek:*
> *that I may dwell in the house of the LORD*
> *all the days of my life,*
> *to gaze upon the beauty of the LORD*
> *and to seek him in his temple.*
>
> PSALM 27:4

> *Send forth your light and your truth,*
> *let them guide me;*
> *let them bring me to your holy mountain,*
> *to the place where you dwell.*
>
> PSALM 43:3

Finish then Thy new creation,
Pure and spotless may we be;
Let us see Thy great salvation,
Perfectly restored in Thee;
Changed from glory into glory,
Till in heaven we take our place,
Till we cast our crowns before Thee,
Lost in wonder, love, and praise.

Charles Wesley